What Research Says to the Teacher

Nonverbal Communication

SECOND EDITION

by Patrick W. Miller

nea PROFESSIONAL LIBRARY

National Education Association
Washington, D.C.

The Author

Patrick W. Miller is Associate Professor of Practical Arts & Vocational-Technical Education at the University of Missouri, Columbia. He is also the coauthor of *Teacher-Written Student Tests*, published by NEA.

The Advisory Panel

Maridell Fryar, Coordinator of Fine Arts and Speech, Midland Independent School District, Midland, Texas

Dr. Charles M. Galloway, Professor of Education, Ohio State University, Columbus

Dr. Joy H. McClintock, Communications Specialist and Speech/Debate Coach, Seminole Senior High School, Seminole, Florida

Connie Mericle, teacher of Educable Mentally Retarded, Bellevue Senior High School, Bellevue, Ohio

Joan Steen Silberschlag, English and speech teacher, Central High School, Phoenix, Arizona

Dr. Shirley N. Weber, Associate Professor and Chair, Department of Afro-American Studies, San Diego State University, California

Note

The opinions expressed in this publication should not be construed as representing the policy or position of the National Education Association. Materials published as part of the What Research Says to the Teacher series are intended to be discussion documents for teachers who are concerned with specialized interests of the profession.

Acknowledgment

The author wishes to express his sincere gratitude and appreciation to Jean E. Miller for her assistance in preparing this manuscript.

Library of Congress Cataloging-in-Publication Data

Miller, Patrick W.
  Nonverbal communication.

  (What research says to the teacher)
  Bibliography: p.
  1. Nonverbal communication in education—United
States. 2. Interaction analysis in education. I. Title.
II. Series.
LB1027.M467   1986   370.15'3   86–8535
ISBN 0–8106–1072–8

CONTENTS

INTRODUCTION

Communication is an ongoing process of sending and receiving messages that enable humans to share knowledge, attitudes, and skills. Considered to be the major ingredient of education, communication is composed of two dimensions—verbal and nonverbal (97,1).* Nonverbal communication has been defined as communication without words (21, 71, 84, 109, 43, 53, 105, 7, 6, 100, 108). Nonverbal messages include overt behaviors such as facial expressions, eye behavior, touching, and tone of voice; as well as less obvious messages such as dress, posture, and spatial distance between two or more people (85). Without uttering a single word, teacher and students constantly send messages to each other. In fact, they send and receive, consciously and unconsciously, nonverbal cues several hundred times a day (21, 109, 15, 99).

Even when we do not move, we transmit messages by our physique, sex, and skin coloration (P).** "Everything communicates," including material objects, physical space, and time systems (54). Although we can turn off verbal output, we cannot turn off the nonverbal. Even silence speaks (71).

> . . . no matter how one may try, one cannot not communicate. Activity or inactivity, words or silence, all have message value: they influence others and these others, in turn, cannot not respond to these communications and are thus themselves communicating. (I, p. 49)

> He that has eyes to see and ears to hear may convince himself that no mortal can keep a secret. If his lips are silent, he chatters with his fingertips; betrayal oozes out of him at every pore. (Q, p. 94)

Commonly, we learn nonverbal communication shortly after birth and practice and refine it throughout our lives (15, 1, 56). Before language emerges, infant behaviors communicate (9, B). As children we first learn nonverbal expressions by watching and imitating, much as we learn verbal skills (76). Young children know far more than they can verbalize (116, 95), and are generally more adept at reading nonverbal cues than most adults because of their limited verbal skills and their recent reliance on the nonverbal to communicate (72, 71). At approximately one year of age, children use distance, eye contact, gestures, touch, intonation patterns, vocalizing, and smiling to communicate with adults and peers (N). As they develop verbal skills, their nonverbal channels of communication do not cease to exist. Rather, the nonverbal messages become entwined in the total

---

*Numbers in parentheses appearing in the text refer to the Bibliography beginning on page 27.

**Letters in parentheses appearing in the text refer to the Selected Resources for the Second Edition on page 32.

communication process (129). These learnings are fundamental because emotional meanings may be communicated through nonverbal channels (61).

Humans use nonverbal communication for the following reasons:

1. *Words have limitations.* Although through the use of words we are able to communicate far better than many animals, there are still numerous areas where we communicate more effectively nonverbally. For example, most of us find it difficult to explain the shape of something or to give directions without using hand gestures or head nods. Similarly, we express our personalities nonverbally, enabling others to form clear impressions of us, which they ultimately use to direct their responses.

2. *Nonverbal signals are powerful.* Because nonverbal cues primarily express inner feelings, they generally evoke immediate action or response. Verbal messages deal basically with the ouside world; therefore, first we consider the information and then we explore its implications. Action is immediate only when well-trained individuals receive commands or orders.

3. *Nonverbal messages are likely to be more genuine.* Except for facial expressions and tone of voice, we cannot control nonverbal behaviors as easily as spoken words. Moreover, we can control some signals, such as pupil dilation and perspiration, only by modifying the emotional state, which is far more difficult than modifying the body message.

4. *Nonverbal signals can express feelings too disturbing to state.* Social etiquette limits what we can say, but nonverbal cues can communicate our thoughts. In interpersonal relationships, it would be improper to tell other people we don't like them or that we think we are better than they are, both of which sentiments we can express nonverbally. Conveniently, though, if we do not verbalize our feelings, we can freely change our minds without having committed ourselves.

5. *A separate communication channel is necessary to help send complex messages.* In addition to expressing feelings and other personal information, nonverbal actions greatly aid the verbal communication process. Vocal intonation alone tells us when a speaker has finished a sentence, what is most important in the speech, and even when the speech has ended. Listener feedback, if vocalized, would be a hodgepodge of interruptions and doubletalk. A speaker can add enormously to the complexity of the verbal message through simple nonverbal signals (4).

Nonverbal behaviors can be amazingly quick and subtle (105, 69, 56) or very explicit (95, 69); they either support or contradict the verbal message being transmitted (100, 77, 1, 69, 82).

5

Some research in communication suggests that many more feelings and intentions are sent and received nonverbally than verbally (56, 47, 81). It has even been suggested that only 7 percent of a message is sent through words, with the remaining 93 percent sent through facial expressions (55 percent) and vocal intonation (38 percent) (82). Words are accented and punctuated by body movements and gestures, while a myriad of expressions are emitted from the face (86). Thus, nonverbal and verbal messages are intertwined as inseparable parts of human communication.

Why, then, if nonverbal communication is vitally important, has it been so long ignored and greatly underestimated? Probably the most influential deterrent has been the human emphasis on verbal prowess. Other "more primitive" expressions have somehow been considered second class.

It is important to be aware of the dominance of the nonverbal message. If there is incongruity between the verbal and the nonverbal, the nonverbal will win hands down (42, 99). Also, the validity and reliability of verbal messages are checked by our nonverbal actions (123). Again, if a discrepancy exists, the nonverbal will dictate.

> Wise men read very sharply all your private history in your look and gait and behavior. The whole economy of nature is bent on expression. The telltale body is all tongues. Men are like Geneva watches with crystal faces which express the whole movement. (29, p. 409)

Nonverbal Communication in the Classroom

All teachers should be aware of nonverbal communication in the classroom for two basic reasons: (1) to become better receivers of student messages; and (2) to gain the ability to send students positive signals that consequently reinforce learning—and, at the same time, to become more adept at avoiding negative signals that stifle learning (72, 97, I).

Being a good message receiver requires more than just listening to words. Much is communicated by nonverbal means (109), such as feelings and values (37). Thus, to be a good receiver of student messages, the teacher must be attuned to many of these subtle cues (87). Imagine for a moment how difficult it would be to teach a course by telephone. Assessing teaching methods and strategies with the help of the nonverbal dialogue that goes on in the classroom would not be possible. Teachers use smiles, frowns, nodding heads, and other not-so-obvious cues as aids to instructions. They tell them whether to slow down, speed up, or in some other way modify the delivery of instructional material.

. The second reason for becoming familiar with nonverbal communication is to become a better message sender. Just as it is important to be a good receiver, so it is important to develop nonverbal "sending" skills. Not only are teachers often unaware of students' nonverbal behaviors, but they are also oblivious to nonverbal messages they relay to students (95). It has been contended that 82 percent of teacher messages are nonverbal, while only 18 percent are verbal (50). Teachers express enthusiasm, warmth, assertiveness, confidence, or displeasure through their facial expressions, vocal intonation, gestures, and use of space (S). Widely used messages sent by teachers to reinforce or modify student behavior include smiles of approval, winks, scowls, and the "evil eye" (114). In addition, there are many other less common methods of nonverbal communication. Touch, for example, is often overlooked as a means of transmitting a message. A pat on the back can demonstrate approval, whereas a slightly firmer pat on the head might bring a student to attention.

When teachers' verbal messages conflict with their nonverbal messages, students become confused, and this confusion often affects their attitudes and learning. Recent clinical and neurosurgical research indicates that the left hemisphere of the brain is involved primarily in verbal and other analytical functions, while the right hemisphere is responsible for spatial and nonverbal processes (96, 66). If conflicting messages are communicated to these two modes, each hemisphere emphasizes only one of the messages and omits information from the other (99). It is very important that teachers understand this concept. If learning is to take place, students must be able to rely on teachers as a credible source of information (75).

Knowledge is transmitted through effective communication and is nurtured by skillfully sending and receiving messages in a variety of situations (60). Just as academic skills are developed through practice, so, too, must nonverbal behaviors be learned and practiced. These behaviors include fostering positive characteristics, mannerisms, actions, and habits, as well as overcoming negative ones that depress the learning atmosphere (49).

The following suggests a continuum model for judging teacher nonverbal behavior with students. It is based on ten dimensions ranging from encouraging to restricting (39, 40, 41, 44, 45).

DIMENSIONS OF TEACHER NONVERBAL BEHAVIOR

Encouraging		*Restricting*
Congruous	⟷	Incongruous
Responsive	⟷	Unresponsive
Positive Affectivity	⟷	Negative Affectivity
Attentive	⟷	Inattentive
Facilitating	⟷	Unreceptive
Supportive	⟷	Disapproving
Intimate	⟷	Distant
Inclusive	⟷	Exclusive
Free Time	⟷	Restricted Time
Open Space	⟷	Closed Space

Congruous/Incongruous behavior refers to the consistency of verbal and nonverbal elements communicated by the teacher. Congruity occurs when the nonverbal supports and reinforces the verbal message; a mixed message or incongruity exists when there is a discrepancy or contradiction between these two channels.

Responsive/Unresponsive behavior refers to modifications in teacher behavior as a result of student feedback. A responsive act occurs when a teacher's reactions or responses are appropriate to the nonverbal student feedback (for example, altering the instructional delivery pattern because of student misunderstanding of lesson content). Unresponsive acts are identified by the lack of teacher responsiveness to student feedback, either by ignoring or being insensitive to student actions.

Positive/Negative Affectivity refers to the expressions exhibited by the teacher to reinforce student behaviors. Positive affective expressions include warm feelings, high regard, cheerful enthusiasm, and acceptance. Negative affective expressions include aloofness, coldness, low regard, indifference and rejection.

Attentive/Inattentive behavior refers to the teacher's ability to listen to student messages. Attentiveness implies listening with patience and interest; inattentiveness implies disinterest in or failure to encourage the student's verbal or nonverbal behavior.

Facilitating/Unreceptive behavior refers to the teacher's responses to student needs and/or problems. A facilitator encourages students to share problems and responds positively to them. An unreceptive teacher openly ignores or responds inappropriately to a student's question or request.

Supportive/Disapproving behavior refers to actions exhibited by the teacher to reinforce or thwart student behavior or interaction. Supportive teacher behaviors include encouraging and praising; disapproving behaviors express dissatisfaction and discouragement—in some cases seeking to punish student behavior.

Intimate/Distant behavior refers to types of contact between teachers and their students. Intimacy is characterized by the presence of a psychological and physical closeness; distance by the absence of physical contact, by withdrawal, or by "cold" treatment.

Inclusive/Exclusive refers to nonverbal behaviors exhibited by the teacher to include or exclude students. Inclusion is evident when mutual glances and acknowledgment foster communicative exchange. Exclusion suggests a refusal to recognize, or an ignoring of the student's presence.

Free Time/Restrictive Time refers to the use of time with others. This includes not only the quantity, but also the quality, of time.

Open Space/Closed Space refers to travel routes and territorial rights in the classroom. Student accessibility to the space and territories of the school and classroom fosters openness, whereas denying access to these areas restricts.

RESEARCH HIGHLIGHTS

Pygmalion in the Classroom, considered one of the most intriguing and controversial publications in the history of educational research, supports the premise that, in fact, teacher expectations (manifested nonverbally) can foster academic achievement. This classic study involved administering a relatively unknown IQ test to elementary school children in a low socioeconomic area. After testing, prospective teachers received a list of students' names identified as high scorers. In reality, these students were chosen at random, not as a consequence of the test results. The teachers were told to expect a great increase in intellectual performance from them. Ironically, at the end of the school year, these students did make sharp increases on IQ test scores (106).

Obviously, these teachers did not tell students they expected higher performances, but they may have conveyed such messages nonverbally through facial expressions, gestures, touch, spatial relationships (130). These subtle nonverbal expectancy behaviors may have been all the students needed to change their self-image, motivation, or achievement (11).

In another study, volunteers recruited to tutor elementary school children were told the experiment involved testing the psychological effects of lighting, and that they were to present a five-minute lesson on home and family safety. The tutors were also read a statement about the students' abilities, classifying them as bright, control, or dull. After this brief explanation, each tutor was individually led into a room to present the lesson to the elementary child. In fact, the study did not measure the effects of lighting (which was only necessary to videotape the lesson), but rather the effect of their expectancies (conveying preconceived notions about intelligence and motivation) on the tutors' nonverbal behaviors.

After evaluation of the videotapes by trained raters, it was concluded that tutors in the microteaching lesson exhibited patterns of nonverbal behavior toward students classified "bright" that were different from those exhibited toward students serving as the control and students termed "dull." The nonverbal behaviors displayed to "bright" students included touching, close proximity, forward body lean, eye contact, more gestures, approving head nods, and positive facial expressions (11).

Such findings point out the need for teachers to be more conscious about prejudging students before they have had a chance to prove (or improve) themselves. Despite efforts to be unbiased, fair, and just, one may have preconceived opinions about certain students, gained either from colleagues or hearsay. When a student has been labeled a troublemaker, for example, there is a need to be especially alert to nonverbal messages and not be waiting to jump on any misconduct.

Even professionals trained to objectively administer tests can be influenced by the case histories of their subjects. A study attempting to support this premise asked 32 practicing psychologists to evaluate the videotaped administration of an intelligence test to children. Prior to evaluation, each psychologist received a case history suggesting that the child was either bright or dull. Analyses of the psychologists' evaluations showed that these case histories significantly affected their judgments (63).

Physical closeness has also been shown to be a nonverbal component that can affect test performance of certain cultural groups. In a study investigating teacher warmth and physical proximity, a school counselor administred the Wechsler Adult Intelligence Scale to 15 Alaska Native high school students. Giving the tests in the usual fashion, the examiner sat 60 inches from the subject and displayed a businesslike manner. Three weeks later, parts of the test were re-administered with seven students randomly assigned to a nonverbal warmth group and eight students to a nonverbal cold group. In the warmth condition, the examiner sat 30 inches from the subjects, at their level and at right angles to them, and smiled frequently when giving the test. In the cold condition, the examiner remained 80 inches from the subjects, stood, and did not smile. Analyses of changed scores were significant: subjects in the warmth condition gained points and subjects in the cold condition remained constant or lost points (67).

Sheer physical appearance can also influence teacher expectations.

One study asked teachers to evaluate students' intellectual potential based on report card grades, verbal description, and a picture of an attractive or unattractive student. Even though the demographic information was the same for both types of students, teachers evaluated the attractive students more favorably (12). In addition, experimental studies indicate that such expectations can be communicated nonverbally (10), creating many pedagogical implications.

Research has also been completed on the nonverbal behaviors of teachers toward the sex and race of students (O). Both white and Black teachers appear to vary their nonverbal responses depending upon the race and sex of the students involved in the interaction (F, O). These studies support the need to ensure that teachers are sensitive to their own nonverbal behaviors when interacting with students from varying sex and ethnic groups. Additional research indicates that nonverbal communication can be a powerful tool used by teachers of handicapped students. Specific examples of appropriate nonverbal cues for visually-impaired, hearing-impaired, learning-disabled and emotionally-disabled students have been suggested (L).

In another experiment, teachers received a report containing pictures, with names and ages, of both male and female students fictitiously said to be involved in a school disturbance. Previously, adult raters had judged each picture either attractive or unattractive. Each teacher was asked to read the report, evaluate the seriousness of the disturbance, and give a general impression of the student involved. When the disturbance was mild, the physical attractiveness of the student did not affect the teacher's reaction. When the misconduct was severe, however, teachers discerned that the behavior of unattractive boys and girls was chronically antisocial. Ironically, teachers did not usually give this judgment for serious misconduct reported for attractive students. They tended to view the attractive students as normal, and blamed the misbehavior on their having a bad day (19).

The influence of expectation is probably felt through subtle affective behaviors that differ from one student to another, and through the effect of this behavior on students' motivation and relations to figures of authority (A, p. 153).

Without words, teachers communicate how they care about students, what is expected of them, and a great many other things to which they would never verbally admit. Omission of nonverbal behaviors also communicates crystal-clear messages. Consider for a moment teachers who repeatedly provide positive reinforcement to a few selected students; the remaining students also receive feedback—perhaps, in such a case, a negative message (100). Students know when something bothers their teachers, whom they like or dislike, and a surprising amount of other information teachers think they keep to themselves (71, 47, 100, 98).

Be aware, though, that much of the literature on nonverbal communication leaves the impression that all nonverbal cues (such as crossed legs and head nods) have implicit meanings. This impression is erroneous because the meanings depend upon when and where the cues are exhibited (37, 127). Not all nonverbal behavior is significant; in fact, no single gesture conveys a true meaning of a situation (81, 62, 72).

Still in its infancy, nonverbal research has been overshadowed by the popular attention given its old sibling, linguistic research (51). Connoisseurs of the subtleties of the nonverbal behavior of others and self recognize the multidimensionality of nonverbal experiences and analyze these cues within the context of various settings (37). Increasing our awareness of our own nonverbal behavior requires practice and patience. As we work to improve nonverbal actions, our goal should be to foster positive characteristics, mannerisms, actions, and habits as well as to overcome negative ones that depress an atmosphere for learning (88).

AREAS OF NONVERBAL EXPRESSION

Facial Expressions

The old adage "A picture is worth a thousand words" well describes what is meant by facial expression.

Facial appearance—including baldness, gray hair, wrinkles, muscle tone, skin coloration, and eye color—offers enduring cues that reveal information about one's age, sex, race, possibly ethnic origins, and status. A less permanent second set of facial cues—including length of hair, hair style, cleanliness, and facial hair—all relate to an individual's concept of beauty. A third group of facial markers are momentary expressions that signal our emotions (58). These expressions are registered by muscle movements that cause changes in the forehead, eyebrows, eyelids, cheeks, nose, lips, and chin (27). Among such examples are raising the eyebrows, wrinkling the brow, curling the lip.

Some facial expressions are readily visible, while others are so fleeting that they go unnoticed (27). Both types can positively or negatively reinforce the spoken word and convey cues concerning emotions and attitude (24, 26, 102). Next to words, then, the human face is the primary source of information for determining an individual's internal feelings (99, 70, 23). However, researchers cannot reach a consensus on the universality of any facial expressions.

Some physiologists contend that the face is capable of producing some 20,000 different expressions (70). Research has indicated that people in our culture display about 33 "kinemes" (individual communicative movements) in the facial area (7).

A man finds room in the few square inches of his face for all the traits of all his ancestors; for the expression of all his history, and his wants. (29, p. 411)

Facial expressions may be involuntary or voluntary. People generally do not think about how to move facial muscles when truly frightened. Thus the facial expression of fear is an example of an involuntary gesture. Facial expressions can also be voluntary, as when an individual wants to deliberately hide his/her feelings. Such expressions are controlled for a number of reasons, but they are often dictated by societal or cultural standards, or are a product of family rules. "Boys should never cry or look afraid" is a rule our society ingrains in its young (27).

Although research indicates that people of all cultures display similar facial cues for some emotions (such as happiness, fear, and surprise), culturally learned rules often trigger different responses. In our culture, for example, a snake might stimulate reactions of fear or disgust. In another culture, however, the same reptile might elicit joy or excitement, as it might represent a culinary delicacy (58).

Often we try to hide feelings and emotions behind masks (28). No matter how sincere they might appear to be, these faces are often directed only by societal norms; they cannot conceal true feelings. The frown, jutting chin, raised eyebrow, open mouth, sneer, are all facial expressions that can betray us and ultimately broadcast our deceptions (24). All of us are capable of faking a happy or sad face, a smile or frown, but the timing inevitably gives us away. We cannot determine how long to keep it on or how quickly to let it go (15). Thus, when trying to deliberately deceive others, we speak at a slower rate, produce more speech errors, exhibit fewer head nods and more smiles (83).

Rosenfeld and his associates at Harvard University introduced a significant contribution to the study of nonverbal communication when they developed the most precise measure, to date, for determining a person's ability to understand facial, body, and vocal cues through 11 different channels of nonverbal communication. In preliminary testing, the Profile of Nonverbal Sensitivity (PONS) ascertained that females were more accurate at interpreting nonverbal cues than males; however, the margin lessened for males in certain occupations such as acting, psychiatry, art, designing, and teaching (104). Further research revealed, to the contrary, that teachers were *not* accurate in interpreting *student* facial cues when considering comprehension of material; it also suggested that teaching experience did not improve the ability to assess the nonverbal cues (64, 65).

A more specific instrument, the Facial Affect Scoring Technique (FAST), was developed and used to show the extent to which observers can recognize (decode) facial expressions of emotion. In both the theory and the instrument, the face was divided into three areas: upper—brows and forehead; middle—eyes, lids, and bridge of nose; and lower—chin, mouth, nose, and cheek. Combining the areas rather than considering individual components provided more precise information (25).

Eyes

The most dominant and reliable features of the face, the eyes provide a constant channel of communication (62). They can be shifty and evasive, conveying hate, fear, and guilt, or they can express confidence, love, and support (81).

> An eye can threaten like a loaded and leveled gun, or can insult like hissing or kicking; or, in its altered mood, by beams of kindness, it can make the heart dance with joy. (29, p. 409)

Often referred to as the "mirrors of the soul," the eyes serve as the major decision factor in deciphering the spoken truth.

> The eyes of men converse as much as their tongues, with the advantage that the ocular dialect needs no dictionary, but is understood all the world over.

When the eyes say one thing, and the tongue another, a practiced man relies on the language of the first. (29, p. 410)

Unlike other parts of the face, eyes can both send and receive messages (62). Except for extremely shy individuals, most people look for social acceptance by studying the eyes of others (81).

Eyes can also accurately indicate a positive or negative relationship. People tend to look longer and more often at those whom they trust, respect, and care about than at those whom they doubt or dislike (59, 85, 100, 20). Thus, eye contact is more evident with people around whom we feel comfortable than with those around whom we feel uneasy. Normal eye dilation is not under the control of the individual (58). But when looking at something pleasing, an individual's pupils will measurably dilate; when viewing something displeasing, the pupils will constrict (4). Personality characteristics such as introversion/extroversion may also influence eye behavior (70).

Eye contact can be manipulated, however, to open or close channels of communication. Most hitchhikers, for example, realize that lengthening eye contact increases their chances of getting picked up. The restaurant patron needing service also knows the importance of catching the server's eye.

Eyes can be used as a good indicator of interest, or lack thereof, in a conversational topic (81). They can be used to determine whom we talk with, for how long, and about what. In addition, eye behaviors can control conversational roles—who is to speak and who is to listen. Thus, visual cues act as monitoring devices that regulate, coordinate, and control succession of speech. When speaking, we usually maintain eye contact and flash visual signals when we want to emphasize a particular point. When listening, we communicate our level of interest in both topic and speaker by looking (104).

Teachers can have individual contact with every student in the classroom through eye contact (62). Attitudes of intimacy, aloofness, concern, or indifference can be inferred by the way a teacher looks or avoids looking at a student.

The level of credibility and honesty has been found to be related to the amount of eye contact exhibited by a speaker (5). Thus, if a teacher has eye contact with only a selected few alert and interested students, other students might consider this to be biased favoritism (100).

Direct teacher eye contact can also express support, disapproval, or neutrality. Numerous evaluator specialists, for example, suggest that a stern look should be the first form of action taken by a teacher to handle obvious cheaters in a testing situation. This direct eye contact usually serves as a powerful corrective measure in negating the nomadic eyes of the cheating student (30).

Students also quickly learn to understand specific eye behavior communicated by the teacher signifying the ending of a class period, a request for an explanation, and a great number of other messages (45). They know from experience to avoid eye contact when the teacher poses a difficult question. The general rule is to look down at notes or stare at the desk to avoid opening the channels of communication.

Most experienced teachers are aware when students are bored with the subject matter being presented. Students' eyes often signal listening and nonlistening behaviors, thus transmitting subtle messages about their lack of attentiveness. Students who are constantly looking at the wall clock rather than watching and listening to the teacher may be indicating the need for a break, the dullness of the content, or a lack of teacher motivation and preparation. In any case, observation of student eye behavior can be used as a constituent in evaluating teacher performance.

Vocal Intonation

The adage "It is not what we say that counts, but how we say it" reflects the meaning of vocal intonation. Sometimes referred to as "paralinguistics," vocal intonation is probably the most understood (56) and valid area of nonverbal communication (22). It includes a multitude of components (for example, rhythm, pitch, intensity, nasality, and slurring) that elicit the "truth" of a message (59, 17). These vocal variations are fundamental components of expressive oral communication (61). If vocal information contradicts verbal, vocal will dominate (82).

The sound aspects of the voice can convey meaning beyond words, including information about individual attributes such as age, emotional state, or other personality characteristics. In addition, vocal qualities are often influential where prejudices against certain paralinguistic styles are evident, as, for example, a whining child. On the other hand, an unconscious bias of the listening public is a widespread positive prejudice in favor of men with low, deep voices with resonant tones, such as those qualities possessed by most male newscasters (119). Studies have also reported the use of vocal cues as accurate indicators of overall appearance, body type, height (73), and race, education, and dialect region (93).

Paralinguistic cues often reveal emotional conditions. (See Table 1.) Differences in loudness, pitch, timbre, rate, inflection, rhythm, and enunciation all relate to the expression of various emotions (16).

Experimental findings suggest that active feelings, such as rage, are exemplified vocally by high pitch, fast pace, and blaring sound. The more passive feelings, such as despair, are portrayed by low pitch, retarded pace, and resonant sound (17). In addition, stress is often vocalized by higher pitch and words uttered at a greater rate than normal. The reverse (lower pitch, slower word pace) is likely during depression (56).

President Richard Nixon demonstrated the importance of paralinguistic communication when he sent transcripts rather than tapes of presidential

Table 1. CHARACTERISTICS OF VOCAL EXPRESSIONS

Feeling	Loudness	Pitch	Timbre
Affection	Soft	Low	Resonant
Anger	Loud	High	Blaring
Boredom	Moderate to Low	Moderate to Low	Moderately Resonant
Cheerfulness	Moderately High	Moderately High	Moderately Blaring
Impatience	Normal	Normal to Moderately High	Moderately Blaring
Joy	Loud	High	Moderately Blaring
Sadness	Soft	Low	Resonant
Satisfaction	Normal	Normal	Somewhat Resonant

*From *The Communication of Emotional Meaning* by J. R. Davitz (p. 63). Copyright © 1964 McGraw-Hill Book Company. Used with the permission of McGraw-Hill Book Company.

CONTAINED IN THE TEST OF EMOTIONAL SENSITIVITY*

Rate	Inflection	Rhythm	Enunciation
Slow	Steady and Slight Upward	Regular	Slurred
Fast	Irregular Up and Down	Irregular	Clipped
Moderately Slow	Monotone or Gradually Falling	. . .	Somewhat Slurred
Moderately Fast	Up and Down; Overall Upward	Regular	. . .
Moderately Fast	Slight Upward	. . .	Somewhat Clipped
Fast	Upward	Regular	. . .
Slow	Downward	Irregular Pauses	Slurred
Normal	Slight Upward	Regular	Somewhat Slurred

conversations to the House Judiciary Committee in 1974. Committee members, questioning possible impeachment and trying to decide the veracity of the tapes' contents, complained that the "meaning" was not truly communicated because of the absence of voice modifications (59). Thus, vocal information—intonation, tone, stress, length, and frequency of pauses—is lost when speech is written; these two informational systems do not always communicate the same feelings (82).

Ironically, the same words or phrases can have many different meanings, depending on how we say them. Let's analyze the phrase, "Thank you." If sincere, it generally means an expression of gratitude, but if intoned sarcastically, it can insinuate an entirely opposite intention. Or when a mother asks a child to apologize for some wrongdoing, she often stresses that the the child "mean it." Thus, the mother expects more than the mere words, "I'm sorry," and listens closely for vocal intonation to support the sincerity of the message.

This powerful nonverbal tool can also readily affect student participation. Consider a classroom situation where the teacher asks a question and calls on one of the more talented students, who in turn answers the question correctly. Generally, the teacher responds with some positive verbal reinforcement enhanced by vocal pitch or tone, expressing the acceptance and liking of the student's answer (often accompanied by a smile or other forms of nonverbal approval). In the same situation, if the teacher called on a less talented student whose response was incorrect, not only might the teacher verbally reject the response, but he or she might also modify the future responding behavior of the less talented student because of the accompanying vocal cues.

Touching

Touching is an important aspect of our culture. Even a handshake will tell us much about another individual's character (81). The human skin has hundreds of thousands of submicroscopic nerve endings, serving as tactual receptors and detecting pressure, temperature, texture, pain, stroking, tickling (70).

Considered by many to be the most primitive form of communication (15), tactual sensitivity begins in childhood with a baby's first cuddling by its mother, and greatly contributes to the mental and emotional adjustment of the individual (70). In fact, traditional methods of birth are a shock because of the "coldness" of moving the infant from a warm, secure womb to a sanitary bassinet. This sudden assault after removal from the mother's body may be a serious mistake (90). New methods, such as Lamaze, that provide gentler transitions foster natural birth and emphasize the importance of touching. Infants touch themselves; they find comfort in the feel of their blankets and excitement in things warm and cold, smooth and rough (32).

Parents transmit feelings to an infant physically, not verbally. A parent can say to a baby, "I love you," but the words do not communicate. Babies are unable to talk and to understand words, but they can communicate most effectively and meaningfully what they feel. During these early stages of development parents must provide total loving and affection through tactual communication (104). The behavioral development of babies deprived of such experiences can be stunted (81), and a variety of health problems (such as allergies and eczema) can result (90).

As infants grow older, they still use tactual experiences as a primary awareness tool to discover and learn until societal inhibitions are imposed to curtail or alter these behaviors (32). Until 10 to 12 years of age, children touch parents to express affiliation or aggression. At adolescence, touching is reduced to the extent that little of it occurs between parent and child beyond their hands and arms (4).

In general, the meaning of touching differs depending on the situation, culture, sex, and age (124). For adults in our culture, touching, in most cases, is taboo. Because tactual experiences are considered private, adults often go out of their way to avoid making physical contact with strangers. Our nontouching society directly relates to our concept of self; we feel that our bodies and clothing are "off limits" except under certain socially accepted conditions. These include sexual encounters with one's spouse; touching between parents and children up to adolescence; greetings and farewells with friends and relatives (handshakes and hugs); professional touching by doctors, dentists, tailors; and contacts in specifically designed encounter groups where the primary purpose is therapy (4).

In most human relationships, touching can give encouragement, express tenderness, and show emotional support. In our culture we often use touch as a symbol of socioeconomic status—superiors may touch inferiors, but the reverse is not likely (59, 15). For this reason, touching in a classroom situation becomes a delicate matter. Since teachers are considered superiors in the classroom, they often initiate touching behaviors. Teacher judgment is the best indicator. A teacher who grabs the arm or shoulder of an unruly student enters the student's space uninvited. Aside from embarrassment, the student may develop other negative feelings toward the teacher. More positively, however, touching can also be used as a reinforcer. At times, a teacher can develop a closer relationship with students by invading their space. A simple pat on the back for a job well done is a much used and usually accepted form of praise. One study reports that when teachers exhibit such behaviors as touching and close body distance, as well as smiles of approval, small children tend to learn significantly more (68). As children grow older, however, these touching behaviors become less appropriate.

Body Postures and Movements

Kinesics refers to body movements (7) and movements communicate meaning (74). Our bodies elucidate true messages about our feelings that cannot be masked. We communicate by the way we walk, stand, and sit (58). When happy, we tend to walk vigorously; conversely, when "down in the dumps," we often slouch or possibly drag our feet (81). The power of body movements and postures is exemplified in foreign movies where English words are dubbed. No matter how well the words are synchronized with lip movement, the gestures and body movements are often awkward. The body tends to move in harmony with words. As they converse with each other, people are often in unison—frequently with similar postural configurations (91).

We express attitudes toward ourselves and others vividly through body motions and posture. Experimental findings indicate that postural relaxation of torso and limbs can denote status or strength in a relationship. One tends to be more relaxed with friends or when addressing an individual of lower status, and less relaxed with strangers or when addressing an individual of superior status (85). Body orientation (the degree to which the communicator's legs and shoulders are in the direction of, rather than away from, the listener) also serves as an indicator of status or liking of the other individual. More direct orientation is related to a more positive attitude (85).

Because gestures are often comprehended more quickly than speech, they are therefore preferred when communication is essential, as in moments of stress. In addition, because such avenues of communication are visual, they travel much farther than spoken words and are unaffected by the presence of noise that interrupts or cancels out speech. Sometimes referred to as emblems, they can either add to or replace words (119).

Although the human body is fashioned similarly throughout the world, postural differences vary tremendously from culture to culture. While there are over one thousand different steady postures available to humans, the postural choices made are usually determined by cultural influences (70). People in our culture have a narrow postural vocabulary and therefore have a difficult time accepting postural ranges found in foreign lands (91). For example, 25 percent of the world's population prefers to squat rather than to sit in chairs, which is an awkward position for us to accept. Supporting this theory:

> Insofar as we know, there is no body motion or gesture that can be regarded as a universal symbol. (7, p. 81)

Body postures and movements are frequently indicators of self-confidence, energy, fatigue, or status (58). In the classroom, students keen to receive body messages of enthusiasm or boredom about the subject matter being taught, can sense confidence or frustration from the unconscious behaviors teachers exhibit. Observant teachers can also tell when students understand the content presented or when they have trouble grasping the major concepts. A student slouching sends a very different message from one leaning forward or sitting erect.

Body movements and postures alone have no exact meaning, but they can greatly support or reject the spoken word (81). If these two means of communication are dichotomized and contradict each other, the result will be a distorted image and most often the nonverbal will dominate.

Dress

Charles Darwin refuted the notion that humans wear clothing mainly for protection from the elements (34). Often dictated by societal norms, the clothing we wear indicates a wide amount of information about ourselves. It identifies sex, age, socioeconomic class, status, role, group membership, personality or mood, physical climate, and time in history (104). Although most of us are only superficially aware of the attire of others, clothing does communicate. Colors and fabrics are coordinated to send messages just as words are put together to form sentences (34). Dress can either alienate or persuade. Appropriate dress is a method of expressing respect for both the particular situation and the people in it: hence the need for Sunday clothes, work clothes, etc. Overtly, as with the hippies of the 1960s and 1970s, attire can be used to demonstrate dissension or refusal to accept the status game (15).

Traditionally, dress was used to classify the sexes (34). In addition, distinctive costumes were worn to indicate rigid hierarchical groups (122). Today's changing Western culture does not follow these "tagging patterns." Historical dress once used to denote gender categories has been challenged by such styles as the female pantsuit. The business suit, once meant for the executive only, is now the appropriate dress for most of the business world. Clothing can also be age-graded. Some garments such as the miniskirt and bikini are appropriate for younger women and seldom worn by older women.

Much research has been completed about the effect of clothing on others. Clothing can reflect the personality, attitudes, and values of the wearer. Some people use clothing for decoration and self-expression; others are concerned with economy or comfort (58). Generally those who prefer dark colors and saturated tones are regarded as outgoing, sociable, and forward. Those who prefer small patterned fabrics are characterized as wanting to make a good impression. Thus, self-expression and ideal self-image are often vividly expressed by the selection of clothing (13).

Another study, attempting to discern variants in impression formation, indicated that photographic female figures with makeup, brightly colored dress, and high hemlines were perceived as sophisticated, immoral, or physically attractive by both sexes (particularly the male population). Such

21

results imply that dress has a decided influence on impressions formed by others, especially the opposite sex (57).

The personal artifacts (makeup, jewelry, glasses) with which we choose to adorn ourselves also communicate a message to others. Glasses, for example, have stereotypically implied intelligence, honesty, and industriousness (120). More recent studies, however, have shown them to convey religiousness, conventionality, and little imagination (57).

An interesting study examined female subjects' descriptions of the characteristics of "popular women." Clothing was found to be second in importance to personality, and physical appearance, which is obviously altered by clothing, was third (125).

Because clothing affects others' perceptions of us, we often dress to "fit the part." These clothing cues, however, have very little effect on people with whom we are familiar. Thus, if we overtly alter our style of dress, people who know us usually think it a "mood,"rather than a permanent change of personality or values (104).

We can consider our attire in theatrical terms. For example, the teacher (actor) must be costumed to fit the curriculum (play) and the classroom (setting). In order to establish credibility, the teacher should strive to appear comfortable and at ease in the role, thus removing some of the typical teacher/student barriers (80). Although outward appearance does not of course indicate one's knowledge, values, or philosophy, dress can communicate; but in most cases, it is only a veneer. Students see instructors based on their motivation, sincerity, and fairness; they will be fooled only momentarily by clothing. A Savile Row suit or Givenchy dress cannot turn a grouch into a lively, dynamic teacher. A smile is worth many times whatever one might pay for clothes (48).

Use of Space

A subtle component of nonverbal communication, the use of space, or proxemics, indicates territory to which we allow or deny access to other people or objects (32, 52). Hall identified three types of space:

1. *Fixed-feature space* (immovable walls or partitions and objects)
2. *Semi-fixed-feature space* (big objects, such as chairs and tables)
3. *Informal space* (personal space around individuals) (52).

The findings and implications of a controlled experiment conducted 30 years ago remain relevant to many classroom environments in today's schools. The study dealt with the effect of different aesthetic room qualities on students' rating of pictured faces based on dimensions of "energy" and "well-being." Subjects were placed in one of three rooms—one beautiful, one ugly, and one average. The beautiful room had two large windows with drapes, beige walls, indirect overhead lighting, and attractive furnishings; the ugly room had two half-windows, battleship gray walls, an overhead bulb with a dirty lampshade, and furnishings to give the impression of a dirty storeroom; the average room (a professor's office) had three windows with shades, battleship gray walls, indirect overhead lighting, and reasonably attractive furnishings. Subjects in the beautiful room rated the faces significantly higher than did subjects in either of the other two rooms. Subject responses in the average room more closely resembled those in the ugly room than those in the beautiful room (79).

A followup study to determine if the results were long-lasting increased subjects' time in both the beautiful and ugly room from the original ten minutes to eight hours (four one-hour sessions and two two-hour sessions). The findings were dramatic: subjects in the ugly room had reactions of monotony, fatigue, headaches, irritability and hostility; while those in the beautiful room responded favorably with feelings of comfort, pleasure, importance, and enjoyment for completing the assigned tasks (89).

The implications concerning fixed-feature spatial environments for today's classrooms are obviously important, considering that students spend about six hours a day, five days a week, forty weeks a year in these learning environments (103). Clearly, the physical classroom environment can create moods and establish how much interaction (communication) takes place (104).

Physical arrangement of furniture, such as chairs, desks, and tables, also dictates spatial boundaries and effectively communicates through subtle channels (113, 103). Most schools lack imagination and creativity regarding the elements that could easily be manipulated to make the learning environment more exciting (103). Despite many teaching innovations, most classroom settings remain approximately the same (117), with dark and dismal interiors (54, 69). Space in the classroom may also serve to indicate status, dominance, and leadership. A teacher's desk may act as a barricade to prevent students from entering her/his space, and thus inhibit interaction (75). Students frequently use space to send a message about their interest or preparation in a course by sitting in the front or back of the classroom.

Researchers have found that straight-row seating, originally evolved to make optimum use of natural lighting from windows (112), greatly affects student involvement in the process of communication. The location of students in typical straight-row seating is a major factor in determining which students the teacher talks with and which students respond to the teacher (2, 112). With such an arrangement, student interaction is greatest in the front and middle row, whether seating is imposed or self-selected (112).

A two-phased experimental study concluded that seating arrangements can also affect test performance. In the first phase of this experiment, 58 undergraduate students were allowed to choose their own seats in a classroom. Analyses of two tests administered to this group showed that students seated at the front of the classroom scored higher than those seated at the rear. In the second phase, 32 of the original group of students were selected and assigned seats in the classroom. After a lecture, students took an announced "pop" quiz based on the lecture content. Again, results showed that students seated at the front of the classroom performed better than those at the rear. High-ability students also performed well, regardless of their position in the classroom. However, low-ability students who were seated at the front of the classroom improved their performance (4). Additional research cautions that this "front and center" area in classroom seating arrangements may not be as important as earlier believed, because other factors influence teacher-student interaction (S).

From childhood we have learned the meanings of thousands of spatial cues (53). Most people in our culture have been reared with the understanding that a precise amount of space must exist when two people communicate. This personal "space bubble" changes size and shape, depending on the situation. Four categories of informal space have been established by our society's middle-class:

1. *Intimate*—This zone is reserved for close relationships, sharing, protecting, and comforting.

2. *Personal*—Informal conversations between friends occur in this 1½-to-4-foot zone.

3. *Social*—An extended distance of 4 to 12 feet is generally acceptable for interaction between strangers, business acquaintances, and teachers and students.

4. *Public*—Between 12 and 25 feet is the distance used for such one-way communication as exhibited by lecturers (52).

It might be noted that in an average arranged classroom, teachers and students are separated by 12 or more feet (36).

Whereas other cultures rely heavily on close proximity to decipher truth and honesty, our culture does not accept closeness except for intimate relationships. From early childhood, we have been taught to avoid body contact with strangers (53). Many nonverbal cues such as eye contact, body gestures, and facial expressions limit the space between individuals. Most of us tend to get closer to those we like, and maintain a greater distance from those we dislike or fear or who are in a superior status position (52, 85, 126). We also stand farther away from people with handicaps, people from different racial backgrounds, and authority figures (104).

The distance between teacher and students is a critical factor in the communication process. Teachers can easily transmit feelings of acceptance or rejection simply by the distance they maintain. They have "freedom of space" whereas students do not (113). Teachers, as well as others, have a tendency to "get closer" to students they like. A quick observation of a classroom situation will often identify the teacher's pets, as well as those students the teacher dislikes. To avoid accusations of favoritism, teachers should make a conscious effort to get within the space bubble of *all* students. By traveling freely throughout the classroom, they reinforce the concept of joint ownership (114).

The most advanced curriculum and highest hopes have little chance of success without a supportive physical learning environment (103). In order to foster productive communication in the classroom, teachers must allow for flexible changes that are beneficial for group interaction. It should be noted, however, that appropriate spatial distances and arrangements are limited by a myriad of variables, including the conversational topic, the nature of the relationship, and the physical constraints present in the classroom (101).

With a minimum amount of effort, it is possible to make changes in the classroom that will positively affect the learning environment. Several general guidelines are as follows:

1. The classroom should offer a variety of stimuli.

2. The classroom should provide a secure, comfortable feeling.

3. The classroom should be adapted to fit the activity.

4. The classroom should give some privacy and individuality.

CONCLUSION

If effective communication is to be achieved in today's schools, it must be an open process where teachers and students possess the ability to accurately send and receive messages. A good teacher is a good listener, not only to words being spoken, but also to silent messages signaling agreement/disagreement, attention/inattention, boredom/interest, and the desire of the student to be heard. Teacher effectiveness is generally characterized by showing enthusiasm, varying facial expressions, gesturing for emphasis, moving toward students, spending more time in front of the class than behind a desk or at the chalkboard, maintaining eye contact, displaying head nods, speaking with clear voice and varied intonation, correlating verbal and nonverbal messages, and exhibiting a sense of humor (128).

To avoid any dogmatic evaluation of students' nonverbal behaviors, one final point needs to be made. No formalized reliable method has been developed that can be used to identify and interpret all nonverbal behaviors (21). Many student behaviors are autonomic, idiosyncratic, and ambiguous when considered out of context (110, 69, 71, 56, T, S). Thus it is important not to jump to conclusions or make generalizations without considering three validity checks on nonverbal communication: (1) deviant behavior from a baseline, (2) cultural backgrounds, and (3) sex differences (22).

Deviant behavior refers to acts that vary from a standard pattern. For instance, it is more important to notice when students who are consistently good responders in the classroom are not following their usual pattern of frantically raising their hands to be heard than to notice that they raise their hands more often than others. The lack of attempts to respond may convey more meaning than the usual hand raising. The critical point is not noticing the frequency of behavior, but, rather, identifying the discrepancies.

The second validity check on nonverbal communication considers the individual's specific culture. Nonverbal behaviors and their perceptions differ in many cultures (94). The ability to read or speak a foreign language does not guarantee an understanding of the cultural aspects that go beyond the lexical (91). What is correct in one country may not be considered appropriate in another (127, 7). Teachers, administrators, and counselors must make personal adjustments to compensate for the cultural diversity found in classrooms. Obviously, cross-cultural differences found in Florida classrooms will not be the same as those found in New York classrooms. Those who teach or work in such culturally pluralistic situations need to become equipped with knowledge and empathy in order to correctly interpret the meaning of these nonverbal differences (51).

The third validity check on nonverbal communication considers students' sex differences. Because of stereotyped upbringing of boys and girls, many nonverbal cues and behaviors can be misinterpreted. Treated differently from birth, boys and girls begin to act differently in some ways. Research has shown that while males are believed to be more aggressive, athletic, and mechanical than females, females are thought to be more conforming, quiet, and generally interested in scholarly activities (78). Teachers may, however, notice in some girls an aggressiveness that can be related to increased participation in sports competition. And it is not at all uncommon to find boys who are more interested in science or music than in sports activities.

Singly, nonverbal behaviors may not have implicit meaning. They should be considered in context (56, 37, 107, 8, T, S). Although some nonverbal actions may be given more weight than others, oversimplifying their analysis should be avoided (70). Nonverbal awareness implies a conscious effort to employ all the senses in receiving and sending messages. Insights into nonverbal communication not only heighten sensitivity to others, but inevitably strengthen self-understanding as well. Certainly, understanding and using nonverbal behavior are important components of good communication between teachers and students.

BIBLIOGRAPHY

1. Achilles, C. M., and French, R. L. "The Case for Nonverbal Communication: Some Assumptions and Research Ideas." In *Inside Classrooms: Studies in Verbal and Nonverbal Communication,* edited by C. M. Achilles and R. L. French. Danville, Ill.: Interstate Printers and Publishers, 1977. ED 143046
2. Adams, R. S., and Biddle, B. *Realities of Teaching and Exploration with Video Tape.* New York: Holt, Rinehart and Winston, 1970.
3. Amidon, E. J. and Flanders, N. A. *The Role of the Teacher in the Classroom.* Minneapolis, Minn. Association for Productive Teaching, 1967.
4. Argyle, M. *Bodily Communication.* New York: International Universities Press, 1975.
5. Beebe, S. "Eye Contact: A Nonverbal Determinant of Speaker Credibility." *Speech Teacher* 23, no. 1 (January 1974): 21–25.
6. Beier, E. G. "Nonverbal Communication: How We Send Emotional Messages." *Psychology Today* 8, no. 5 (October 1974): 53–56.
7. Birdwhistell, R. L. *Kinesics and Context.* Philadelphia: University of Pennsylvania Press, 1970.
8. Bremme, D. W., and Erickson, F. "Relationships Among Verbal and Nonverbal Classroom Behaviors." In *Theory into Practice,* 16, no. 3 (June 1977), edited by C. M. Galloway; 153–61.
9. Bullowa, M. "Linguistics: Infant Speech from Nonverbal Communication to Language." *Journal of Learning Disabilities* 10, no. 6 (June/July 1977): 354–55.
10. Chaikin, A. L., and others. "Students' Reactions to Teachers' Physical Attractiveness and Nonverbal Behavior: Two Exploratory Studies." *Psychology in the Schools* 15, no. 4 (October 1978): 588–95.
11. Chaikin, A. L.; Sigler, E.; and Derlega, V. J. "Nonverbal Mediators of Teacher Expectancy Effects." *Journal of Personality and School Psychology* 30, no. 1 (1974): 144–49.
12. Clifford, M. M., and Walster, E. "The Effect of Physical Attractiveness on Teacher Expectation." *Sociology of Education* 42, no. 2 (Spring 1973): 248–58.
13. Comption, N. "Personal Attributes of Color and Design Preferences in Clothing Fabrics." *Journal of Psychology* 54 (1962): 191–95.
14. Daum, J. "Proxemics in the Classroom: Speaker-Subject Distance and Educational Performance." Paper presented at annual meeting of Southeastern Psychological Association, 1972.
15. Davis, F. *Inside Intuition,* New York: New American Library, 1973.
16. Davitz, J. R. *The Communication of Emotional Meaning.* New York: McGraw-Hill Book Co., 1964.
17. _____, and Davitz, L. J. "Nonverbal Vocal Communication of Feeling." *Journal of Communication* 11, no. 2 (June 1961): 81–86.
18. Dewey, J. *The Child and the Curriculum.* Chicago: University of Chicago Press, 1902.
19. Dion, K. "Social Desirability and the Evaluation of a Harm-doer." Doctoral dissertation, University of Minnesota, 1970. *Dissertation Abstracts International* 32, (1970): 534A.
20. Drecksel, D. "Nonverbal Communication: Toward Interaction Analysis." Paper presented at annual meeting of Western Speech Communication Association, Phoenix, Arizona, November 22-23, 1977. ED 149392
21. Dunning, G. B. "Research in Nonverbal Communication." In *Theory into Practice* 10, no. 4 (October 1971), edited by J. R. Frymier; 250–58.
22. Eckman, B. "Making Valid Nonverbal Judgments." *English Journal* 66, no. 8 (November 1977): 72–74.
23. Ekman, P., and Friesen, W. V. "Head and Body Cues in the Judgment of Emotion: A Reformulation." *Perceptual and Motor Skills* 24, no. 3 (June 1967): 711–24.
24. _____, and _____ "Constants Across Cultures in the Face and Emotion." *Journal of Personality and Social Psychology,* 17, no. 2 (1971): 124–29.

25. _____ ; _____ ; and Tomkins, S. S. "Facial Affect Scoring Technique: A First Validity Study." *Semiotica* 3 (1971): 37–58.

26. _____ ; _____ ; and Ellsworth, P. *Emotions in the Human Face*. New York: Pergamon Press, 1972.

27. _____ , and _____ . *Unmasking the Face*. Englewood Cliffs, N.J.: Prentice Hall, 1975.

28. _____ , and _____ . "Detecting Deception from the Body or Face." *Journal of Personality and Social Psychology* 219, no. 3 (1974): 288–98.

29. _____ Emerson, R. W. *The Prose Works of Ralph Waldo Emerson,* vol. 2. Boston: James R. Osgood and Co., 1873.

30. Erickson, R. C., and Wentling, T. L. *Measuring Student Growth: Techniques and Procedures for Occupational Education*. Boston: Allyn and Bacon, 1976.

31. Ernst, F. *Who's Listening?* Vallejo, Calif.: Address Set, 1968.

32. Fast, J. *Body Language*. New York: M. Evans and Co., 1970.

33. Ferguson, E. S. "The Mind's Eye: Nonverbal Thought in Technology." *Educational Horizons* 57, no. 1 (Fall 1978), 42–46.

34. Fowles, J. "Why We Wear Clothes." *ETC: A Review of General Semantics* 31, no. 4 (December 1974): 343–52.

35. Fredrickson, P. A. K., and Ertel, K. A. "Analysis of Student Perceptions of Typewriting Teacher Nonverbal Behavior." *Delta Epsilon Journal* 14, no. 4 (October 1977): 7–15.

36. French, R. L. "Building Student Involvement Through Nonverbal Communication." *Tennessee Education* 2, no. 27 (Summer 1972): 5–9.

37. _____ . "Teaching the Nonverbal Experience." In *Theory into Practice* 16, no. 3 (June 1977), edited by C. M. Galloway; 176–82.

38. Freud, S. "Fragment of an Analysis of a Case of Hysteria" (1905). In *Collected Papers,* 3, New York: Basic Books, 1959.

39. Galloway, C. M. "Nonverbal Communication." *Instructor* 77, no. 8 (April 1968): 37–42.

40. _____ . *Nonverbal Communication: A Needed Focus,* 1968. ED 025484

41. _____ . "Nonverbal Communication." In *Theory into Practice* 7, no. 5 (December 1968), edited by J. R. Frymier; 172–75.

42. _____ . "The Challenge of Nonverbal Research." In *Theory into Practice* 10, no. 4 (October 1971), edited by J. R. Frymier; 310–14.

43. _____ . "Nonverbal: The Language of Sensitivity." In *Theory into Practice* 10, no. 4 (October 1971), edited by J. R. Frymier; 227–30.

44. _____ . "The Nonverbal: An Approach for Supervisors." Paper presented at Supervision of Instruction Symposium 2: Observation Systems and the Supervisor, January 1972. ED 064800

45. _____ . *An Analysis of Theories and Research on Nonverbal Communication*. Washington, DC: ERIC Clearinghouse on Teacher Education, February 1972.

46. _____ . *Silent Language in the Classroom*. Bloomington, Ind.: Phi Delta Kappa Education Foundation, 1976.

47. _____ . "Nonverbal: Authentic or Artificial." In *Theory into Practice* 16, no. 3 (June 1977), edited by C. M. Galloway; 129–33.

48. Gariepy, D. *Manage Your Way to Success*. Ware, Mass.: J. A. M. Publishing Co., 1970.

49. Garner, W. C. "Nonverbal Communication and the Teacher." *School and Society*. 98, no. 2327 (October 1970): 363–64.

50. Grant, B. M., and Hennings, D. G. *The Teacher Moves: An Analysis of Nonverbal Activity*. New York: Teachers College Press, 1971.

51. Grove, C. L. *Nonverbal Behavior, Cross-Cultural Contact, and the Urban Classroom Teacher*. New York: ERIC Clearinghouse on the Urban Disadvantaged, 1976. ED 120275

52. Hall, E. T. *The Hidden Dimension*. Garden City, N.Y.: Doubleday, 1969.

53. _____ . *The Silent Language*. New York: Doubleday, 1973.

54. _____ , and Hall, M. R. "Nonverbal Communication for Educators." In *Theory into Practice* 16, no. 3 (June 1977), edited by C. M. Galloway; 141–44.

55. Halpin, A. W. "Muted Language." *School Review* 68, no. 1 (Spring 1960): 85–104.

56. Hamersma, R. J., and Mark, R. "Importance and Use of Nonverbal Communication." *Texas Personnel and Guidance Journal* 5, no. 1 (Spring 1977): 7–16.

57. Hamid, P. N. "Style of Dress as a Perceptual Cue in Impression Formation." *Perceptual and Motor Skills*, 26, no. 3 (1968): 904–06.

58. Harrison, R. P. *Beyond Words: An Introduction to Nonverbal Communication.* Englewood Cliffs, N.J.: Prentice-Hall, 1974.

59. Henley, N. M. *Body Politics.* Englewood Cliffs, N.J.: Prentice-Hall, 1977.

60. Hennings, D. G. *Mastering Classroom Communication.* Pacific Palisades, Calif.: Goodyear Publishing Co., 1975.

61. _____. "Learning to Listen and Speak." In *Theory into Practice* 16, no. 3 (June 1977), edited by C. M. Galloway; 183–88.

62. Hodge, R. L. "Interpersonal Classroom Communication Through Eye Contact." In *Theory into Practice* 10, no. 4. (October 1971), edited by J. R. Frymier; 264–67.

63. Jacobs, J., and DeGraaf, C. "Expectancy and Race: Their Influences upon the Scoring of Individual Intelligence Tests." Paper presented at annual meeting of American Educational Research Association, 1973. ED 068529

64. Jecker, J. D.; Maccoby, N.; and Breitrose, H. S. "Improving Accuracy in Interpreting Nonverbal Cues of Comprehension." *Psychology in the Schools* 2, no. 3 (1965): 239–44.

65. _____; _____; _____; and Rose, E. "Teacher Accuracy in Assessing Cognitive Visual Feedback from Students." *Journal of Applied Psychology* 48, no. 6 (1964): 363–97.

66. Key, M. R. *Nonverbal Communication: A Research Guide and Bibliography.* Metuchen, N.J.: Scarecrow Press, 1977.

67. Kleinfeld, J. *Instructional Style and the Intellectual Performance of Indian and Eskimo Students.* Washington, D.C.: Office of Education, U.S. Department of Health, Education and Welfare, 1972. ED 059831

68. _____. *Using Nonverbal Warmth to Increase Learning: A Cross-Cultural Experiment,* 1973. ED 081568

69. Knapp, M. L. "The Role of Nonverbal Communication in the Classroom." In *Theory into Practice* 10, no. 4 (October 1971), edited by J. R. Frymier; 243–49.

70. _____. *Nonverbal Communication in Human Interaction.* New York: Holt, Rinehart and Winston, 1972.

71. Koch, R. "The Teacher and Nonverbal Communication." In *Theory into Practice* 10, no. 4 (October 1971), edited by J. R. Frymier; 231–42.

72. _____, and Rickman, J. K. "Nonverbal Communication in a Humanistic Program." In *Theory into Practice* 16, no. 3 (June 1977), edited by C. M. Galloway; 192–99.

73. Kramer, E. "The Judgment of Personal Characteristics and Emotions from Nonverbal Properties of Speech." *Psychological Bulletin* 60 (1963): 408–20.

74. Leathers, D. G. *Nonverbal Communication Systems.* Boston: Allyn and Bacon, 1976.

75. Lewis, P. V., and Page, Z. "Educational Implications of Nonverbal Communication." *ETC: A Review of General Semantics* 31, no. 4 (December 1974): 371–75.

76. Longfellow, L. "Body Talk: The Game of Feeling and Expression." *Psychology Today* 4, no. 5 (October 1971): 45–46.

77. Love, A. M., and Roderick, J. A. "Teacher Nonverbal Communication: The Development and Field Testing of an Awareness Unit." In *Theory into Practice* 10, no. 4 (October 1971), edited by J. R. Frymier; 295–99.

78. Maccoby, E. *The Development of Sex Differences.* Stanford, Calif.: Stanford University Press, 1966.

79. Maslow, A., and Mintz, N. "Effects of Aesthetic Surroundings: Initial Effects of Those Surroundings upon Perceiving 'Energy' and 'Well-Being' in Faces." *Journal of Psychology* 41 (1956): 247–54.

80. McCroskey, J.; Richmond, V.; and Daly, J. "Toward the Measurement of Perceived Homophily in Interpersonal Communication." Paper presented at annual meeting of International Communication Association, 1974. ED 094433

81. McGough, E. *Your Silent Language.* New York: William Morrow and Co., 1974.

82. Mehrabian, A. "Communication Without Words." *Psychology Today* 2, no. 4 (September 1968): 53–55.

29

83. _____. "Nonverbal Betrayal of Feelings." *Journal of Experimental Research in Personality* 5, no. 1 (March 1971): 64–73.

84. _____. *Silent Messages.* Belmont, Calif: Wadsworth Publishing Co., 1971.

85. _____. *Nonverbal Communication.* Chicago: Aldine-Atherton, 1972.

86. Melson, G. F. and Hulls, M. J. "The Interplay of Verbal and Nonverbal Communication in Young Children." Paper presented at Annual National Conference on Language Arts in the Elementary School, Phoenix, Arizona, April 22-24, 1977. ED 147793

87. Miller, P. W. "Please Hear What I'm Not Saying," *School Shop* 38, no. 2 (October 1978): 35.

88. _____. "Improving Communication Through What You Don't Say." *VocEd: Journal of the American Vocational Association* 55, no. 6 (June 1980): 22–23.

89. Mintz, N. "Effects of Aesthetic Surroundings: II, Prolonged and Repeated Experiences in a 'Beautiful' and an 'Ugly' Room." *Journal of Psychology* 41 (1956): 459–66.

90. Montagu, A. *Touching: The Human Significance of the Skin.* New York: Columbia University Press, 1971.

91. Morain, G. G. *Kinesics and Cross-Cultural Understanding.* Arlington, Va.: ERIC Clearinghouse on Languages and Linguistics, 1978. ED 157405

92. Morris, D., and others. *Gestures: Their Origins and Distribution.* New York: Stein and Day Publishers, 1979.

93. Nerbonne, G. "The Identification of Speaker Characteristics on the Basis of Aural Cues." Doctoral dissertation, Michigan State University, 1967. *Dissertation Abstracts International* 28 (1967): 4332–33B.

94. Norton, L., and Dobson, R. "Perceptions of Teachers' Nonverbal Behavior by Children of Different Race, Age, and Sex. *Humanist Educator* 14, no. 3 (March 1976): 94–101.

95. Ostler, R., and Kranz, P. L. "More Effective Communication Through Understanding Young Children's Nonverbal Behavior." *Young Children* 31, no. 2 (January 1976): 113–20.

96. Paivio, A. "Language and Knowledge of the World." *Educational Researcher* 3, no. 9 (October 1974): 5–12.

97. Parker, L. R., and French, R. L. "Description of Student Behavior: Verbal and Nonverbal." In *Theory into Practice* 10, no. 4 (October 1971), edited by J. R. Frymier; 276–81.

98. Pietras, T. P. "Teachers' Verbal and Nonverbal Behavior as Indices of Teacher Expectancy." Paper presented at Annual Meeting of American Educational Research Association, Toronto, Canada, March 27-31, 1978. ED 156627

99. Rice, D. R. "Verbal-Nonverbal Communication in the Elementary Science Classroom—A New Perspective." *School Science and Mathematics* 77, no. 7 (November 1977): 563–66.

100. Richey, H. W., and Richey, M. H. "Nonverbal Behavior in the Classroom." *Psychology in the Schools* 15, no. 4 (1978): 571–76.

101. Rollman, S. A. *Nonverbal Communication in the Classroom: An Overview.* Harrisburg, Va.: James Madison University, 1976. ED 150667

102. Rosenfeld, H. M. "Instrumental Affiliative Functions of Facial and Gestural Expressions." *Journal of Personality and Social Psychology* 4, no. 1 (1966): 65–72.

103. Rosenfeld, L. B. "Setting the Stage for Learning." In *Theory into Practice* 16, no. 3 (June 1977), edited by C. M. Galloway; 167–73.

104. _____, and Civikly, J. M. *With Words Unspoken: The Nonverbal Experience.* New York: Holt, Rinehart and Winston, 1976.

105. Rosenthal, R.; Archer, D.; DeMatteo, M. R.; Koivumaki, J.H.; and Rogers, R. L. "Body Talk and Tone of Voice: The Language Without Words." *Psychology Today* 8, no. 4 (September 1974): 64–68.

106. _____, and Jacobsen, L. *Pygmalion in the Classroom.* New York: Holt, Rinehart and Winston, 1968.

107. Ruesch, J., and Kees, W. *Nonverbal Communication.* Los Angeles: University of California Press, 1956.

108. Schlesinger, J. S. "Nonverbal Communication: Information and Application for Counselors." *Personnel and Guidance Journal* 57, no. 4 (December 1978): 183–88.
109. Schneider, J. E. "Mind to Mind Communication: Nonverbal Influence?" In *Theory into Practice* 10, no. 4 (October 1971), edited by J. R. Frymier; 259–63.
110. Schusler, R. A. "Nonverbal Communication in the Elementary Classroom." In *Theory into Practice* 10, no. 4 (October 1971). edited by J. R. Frymier: 282–87.
111. Smith-Hanen, S. S. "Effects of Nonverbal Behaviors on Judged Levels of Counselor Warmth and Empathy." *Journal of Counseling Psychology* 24, no. 2 (1977); 87–91.
112. Sommer, R. *Personal Space: The Behavioral Basis of Design.* Englewood Cliffs, N.J.: Prentice-Hall, 1969.
113. _____. "Classroom Layout." In *Theory into Practice* 16, no. 3 (June 1977), edited by C. M. Galloway; 174–82.
114. Spanjer, A. R. *Teaching Performance: Some Bases for Change.* Salem, Ore.: Oregon ASCD Curriculum Bulletin, April 1972. ED 065463
115. Stewig, J. W. "Nonverbal Communication: 'I See What You Say.'" *Language Arts* 51, no. 2 (February 1979): 150–55.
116. Strom, R., and Ray, W. "Communication in the Affective Domain." In *Theory into Practice* 10, no. 4 (October 1971), edited by J. R. Frymier; 268–75.
117. Taylor, A. P., and Vlastos, G. *School Zone: Learning Environments for Children.* New York: Van Nostrand Reinhold, 1975.
118. Tepper, D. T., and Haase R. F. "Verbal and Nonverbal Communication of Facilitative Conditions." Journal of Counseling Psychology 25, no. 1 (January 1978): 35–42.
119. Thompson, D. S. *Language.* New York: Time-Life Books, 1975.
120. Thornton, G. "The Effect of Wearing Glasses upon Judgments of Persons Seen Briefly." *Journal of Applied Psychology* 28, no. 3 (June 1944): 203–7.
121. Tyler, R. W. *Basic Principles of Curriculum and Instruction.* Chicago: University of Chicago Press, 1950.
122. Veblen. T. *The Theory of the Leisure Class.* New York: A. M. Kelley, Bookseller, 1975.
123. Victoria, J. "A Language for Affective Education." In *Theory into Practice* 10, no. 4 (October 1971), edited by J. R. Frymier; 300–304.
124. Wilkinson, A. M. "Total Communication." *English in Education* 6, no. 3 (Winter 1972): 55–62.
125. Williams, M. C., and Eicker, J. B. "Teenagers' Appearance and Social Acceptance." *Journal of Home Economics* 58, no. 6 (June 1966): 457–61.
126. Wolfgang, A. "Projected Social Distances as a Measure of Approach-Avoidance Behavior Toward Radiated Figures." *Journal of Community Psychology* 1, no. 2 (1973): 226–28.
127. _____. "The Silent Language in the Multicultural Classroom." In *Theory into Practice* 16, no. 3 (June 1977), edited by C. M. Galloway: 145–52.
128. _____. "The Teacher and Nonverbal Behavior in the Multicultural Classroom." In *Nonverbal Behavior: Applications and Cultural Implications,* edited by A. Wolfgang. New York: Academic Press, 1979.
129. Wood, B. S. *Children and Communication: Verbal and Nonverbal Language Development.* Englewood Cliffs, N.J.: Prentice-Hall, 1976.
130. Zuckerman, M., and others. "Accuracy of Nonverbal Communication as Determinant of Interpersonal Expectancy Effects." *Environmental Psychology and Nonverbal Behavior* 2, no. 4 (1978): 206–14.

SELECTED RESOURCES
FOR THE SECOND EDITION

A.   Cooper, H., and Good, T. *Pygmalion Grows Up: Studies in the Expectation Communication Process.* New York: Longman, 1983.

B.   Dil, N. "Nonverbal Communication in Young Children." *Topics in Early Childhood Special Education* 4, no. 2 (1984): 82–99.

C.   Druckman, D., Rozelle, R. M., and Baxter, J. C. *Nonverbal Communication.* Beverly Hills, Calif.: Sage Publications, 1982.

D.   DuBrin, A. J. *Effective Business Psychology.* Reston, Va. Reston Publishing Co., 1985.

E.   Feldman, R. S., ed. *Development of Nonverbal Behavior in Children.* New York, Springer-Verlag, 1982.

F.   Feldman, R. S. "Nonverbal Behavior, Race, and the Classroom Teacher." *Theory into Practice* 24, no. 1 (Winter 1985): 45–49.

G.   Hall, J. A. *Nonverbal Sex Differences.* Baltimore, Md.: Johns Hopkins University Press, 1984.

H.   Hillison, J., and Crunkilton, J. R. "Use of Teacher Nonverbal Cues with Handicapped Students." *Journal for Special Educators* 19, no. 3 (Spring 1983): 1–7.

I.   Hinton, B. E. "Selected Nonverbal Communication Factors Influencing Adult Behavior and Learning." *Lifelong Learning* 8, no. 8. (June 1985): 23–26.

J.   Key, M. R. *Nonverbal Communication Today.* New York, Mauton Publishers, 1982.

K.   Miller, P. W. *Nonverbal Communication: Its Impact on Teaching and Learning.* National Education Association 1983. Filmstrip.

L.   Pearson, J. C. *Gender and Communication.* Dubuque, Iowa: William C. Brown Publishers, 1985.

M.   Poyatos, F. *New Perspectives in Nonverbal Communication.* New York, Pergamon Press, 1983.

N.   Rom, A., and Bliss, L. S. "The Use of Nonverbal Pragmatic Behavior by Language-Impaired and Normal-Speaking Children." *Journal of Communication Disorders* 16, no. 4 (July 1983): 251–56.

O.   Simpson, A. W., and Erickson, M. T. "Teachers' Verbal and Nonverbal Communication Patterns as a Function of Teacher Race, Student Gender, and Student Race." *American Educational Research Journal* 20, no. 2 (Summer 1983): 183–98.

P.   Vargas, M. F. "Studying Nonverbal Communication Through Creative Dramatics." *English Journal* 73, no. 6 (October 1984): 84–85.

Q.   Watzlawick, P.; Beavin, J. H.; and Jackson, D. D. *Pragmatics of Human Communication: A Study of Interactional Patterns, Pathologies, and Paradoxes.* New York: W. W. Norton and Company, 1967.

R.   Williams, J. W., and Eggland, S. A. *Communication in Action.* Cincinnati, Ohio: South-Western Publishing Co., 1985.

S.   Woolfolk, A. E., and Brooks, D. M. "The Influence of Teachers' Nonverbal Behaviors on Students' Perceptions and Performance." *Elementary School Journal* 85, no. 4 (March 1985): 513–28.

T.   _____ and Galloway, C. M. "Nonverbal Communication and the Study of Teaching." *Theory into Practice* 24, no. 1 (Winter 1985): 77–84.